Silent, We Sit

# Silent, We Sit

Poems by Emily Dalgo

Cover Photograph by Bill Kakenmaster
Cover Design by Casey Chiappetta
Illustrations by Jacob Bray
Text Design by Sonia Tabriz

BleakHouse Publishing
2016

# BleakHouse Publishing

Ward Circle Building 254
American University
Washington, DC 20016

NEC Box 67
New England College
Henniker, New Hampshire 03242

www.BleakHousePublishing.com

Robert Johnson – Editor & Publisher
Sonia Tabriz - Managing Editor
Liz Calka - Creative Director

Casey Chiappetta – Chief Operating Officer
Alexa Marie Kelly – Chief Editorial Officer
Emily Dalgo – Chief Development Officer
Rachel Ternes – Chief Creative Officer

Carla Mavaddat – Art Director
Ella Decker – Art Curator

Copyright © 2016 by Emily Dalgo

All rights reserved. No part of this book shall be reproduced or transmitted in any form or by any means, electronic, mechanical, magnetic, photographic including photocopying, recording or by any information storage and retrieval system, without prior written permission of the publisher. No patent liability is assumed with respect to the use of the information contained herein. Although every precaution has been taken in the preparation of this book, the publisher and author assume no responsibility for errors or omissions. Neither is any liability assumed for damages resulting from the use of the information contained herein.

ISBN-13: 978-0-9961162-1-3

Printed in the United States of America

To my mother—

Thank you for giving me my voice and for teaching me how to use it.

# Table of Contents

Acknowledgments

## I
A Haiku - 3
Headlines - 4
Cycle - 6
Security - 7
Solitary - 8
3am Submission - 9
Self-Deprecation - 10
2010 - 12
Afterlife - 13
Desperation - 14
Apathy - 15
Dark Voice - 16
Shift - 17
Rehab - 18
Routine - 19
Buddy - 20
Unwind - 21
Masquerades - 22
Polished Souls - 23
Haiku No. 2 - 24

## II
See More - 27
Half of Me - 28
Resurgence - 30
Timing - 31
Parallel Universe - 32
Queens - 33
Kings - 34
Fade - 35
Inevitable - 36
April Showers - 37
Saying Goodbye - 38
Haiku No. 3 - 39

About the Author
About the Artist and Designers
Other Titles from BleakHouse Publishing
More Praise for *Silent, We Sit*

# Acknowledgments

I would like to thank several members of the BleakHouse Publishing family for their unwavering energy, positivity, and support. Sonia Tabriz patiently formatted a jumbled file of text into a book, provided artistic advice, and challenged me to understand my poetry's aesthetic. Jacob Bray created the striking artwork that introduces each part of this collection, and Casey Chiappetta thoughtfully designed the cover of this book. Thank you both for offering your keen eyes and sophisticated sense of design.

Finally, I would like to thank Professor Robert Johnson. No matter how many times I thank him, words can never capture the deep sense of gratitude I feel for his inspirational presence in my life. Professor Johnson has served as a mentor, confidant, and friend over the past two years. Were it not for him, each line in this book would still be hidden away in private word documents and journals. For believing in me and the message and power of my poetry so sincerely, I thank him most profoundly.

PART I

# A Haiku

I am chained to a
dead animal I keep for-
getting to bury

# Headlines

Your bright smile greets me at 6am
White, shining against your black skin
"Good morning!"
"How are you?"
"I'm doing well."
A smile.
Always a smile,
Teeth, waving hello behind thick lips.

The stacks of newspapers in your arms must be heavy,
As heavy as each letter strung together in each word of each headline,
Announcing another murder, another terror, another fear to be feared

The stacks of newspapers in your hands
Never break your shining smile
Here, at 6am.

I thought about how smart you must be,
Reading the news every morning before you deliver.
You must sit down with coffee and open up the crisp pages,
Feeling like you're cheating the rest of the world—
Your eyes the first to feast.
A messiah delivering the news.

Like an elf in the night,
Filling the racks with stacks of papers
Before we wake.

But as the weeks went by your smile didn't fade
"Hello! Good morning! How are you?"
Eric Garner, Tamir Rice, Michael Brown,
Your smile didn't fade
Baltimore, Mizzou, Ferguson,
Your smile didn't fade

Black Lives Matter, All Lives Matter, I Can't Breathe,
Hands Up Don't Shoot, He Was Unarmed,
He Was Only Twelve, He Was Not A Thug,
He was not a thug, he was not a thug, what is a thug,
What is a thug,
Black skin is not a sin why do my people keep forgetting?
I am ashamed, I don't want this, you don't deserve this,
We don't need this, we can't have this.
Your smile didn't fade.

I thought about how you must not read the news
Because you couldn't be so happy if you read these papers
every day.

# Cycle

No one is left to protect you,
because you've become what we need protection from.
No advocates or witnesses, just prisons that are businesses.
Trading stocks on your life, held against the ground with a knife
Your affidavit: you better engrave it,
on your mind
on your soul, because who you were they'll never know.
What you did, what you said, where you've been: it'll all go
in time, in time. While you do your time.

Your capital offense put freedom in the past tense,
But who gets to decide
if you live or if you die?
Those unknown faces in the crowd—whose eyes watched the clock?
As it ticked toward their liberation and away from yours,
those unknown faces in the crowd,
listened to what they could
although legal jargon allows for little to be understood.
Now no one is left to protect you, or speak on your behalf.
You're beaten and degraded by the security staff.
Punishment consumes you, becomes you.
Odious inclinations, cruel temptations with no explanations,
No justifications.
Grit your teeth shut your eyes clench your fists, for
whatever's going to come.
Because you are who we need
protection from.

# Security

You are my catalyst;
A reason.
Something to believe in.
You are my muse;
An addiction.
Something to breathe in.
You are my impetus;
A spectacle inside my cell,
Classified, safe inside,
With me in this hell.

## Solitary

Pain is tangible
        even in my sleep.
I hear your voice
far away.
        A distant memory
shakes me awake.

These dreams pervade my sleep,
Crippling my unconscious thought.
Leaving me awake, alone; the taste of you still on my tongue.
Let me lie in wonder,
Seeing the forged images again.
Leaving me depressed, alone; the feel of you still on my tongue.

Communication isn't connection
        and as I hear your voice
I am reminded of the loneliness sheltered by my skull,
        my skin.
Night seeps through the cracks
        in droplets of darkness
Swimming, silent
        cold
Distant and alone.
Toes squirming heart pounding
Night seeps through the window and yanks my sheets
        away from me
A metal skeleton
Heavy but hollow
Turning pupils into dilated receptors of pain so palpable
They taste it in each salty blink and
        each twitching stare
At the white ceiling.

# 3am Submission

Depression is loneliness always
Depression is hunger and thirst that isn't satisfied with food or drink
Depression is tired
It is endless hours of sleep
That leave me more exhausted
Depression is darkness
It is absent-minded tears
It is shivering under warm covers
It is the dreams that feel like home
But waking up in a place without feeling
Depression is self-conscious
It is afraid
It is fear
Of failure, of friends, of confrontation
Depression makes forced smiles tremble
And throats close.
It takes away words and replaces them with sighs

# Self-Deprecation

No amount of victory calms you,
hateful one.

Your hot breath irritates my neck, my ears, my eyes as they
narrow in your direction.
I did this; I did this for myself.
"You cheated," you tell me.
Lies.
Embarrassment and hesitation reach from the ground, their
little fingers extended.
Their little hands opening, closing, helpless like a toddler.
You trick me.

I hoist them onto my shoulders and there they become
heavy.

This is when I fall.
The hateful one, the one whose lip is always raised in detest.
The hateful one, the one who shreds the papery walls I build
against you.
The hateful one, the one who laces the praise of others with
painful spices.
Each dose of my happiness is reevaluated. You never agree
to prescribe it.
I sneak away to indulge in deserved appreciation but you
follow me.

You lurk.

You slap my face in your self-induced aching,
your hot breath stings me again.

Regret becomes my name.
My smile dies and suddenly, I have accomplished

nothing.

You tell me:

I am nothing.

I believe you.

## 2010

Lies have no kindness to them,
They are solipsistic instead,
Content with the wasted breath, the shadowed undertones
To cripple the misled.

They do not see longing gazes from devoted eyes,
They do not hear
Heavy heartbeats glugging through the flumes
Natural and clear.

They remain, when they should decay to past,
They stiffen when they should bend.
They use miserly emotion for existence
To which no truth comprehends.

They cannot think of so many smiles to a face
Or of thoughts unmasked.
Their stories are an abrupt struggle to convince
Too tense, or too lax.

They hear in every scramble for protection
A condescending cry.
As like as not, when emerged over their hypocrisy
They should fade to defeated sigh.

# Afterlife

If I choose
to die
Do they still win?
If I choose to
take my life
What will become of the secrets I hold?
of the memories they torture out of my grasp.
will they dissipate into the wind or sea
or do they stay inside, waiting to rot away with me?
will they be locked inside my skull cell always
or will they leap and bound and find the sun's rays?
If I choose to die, will I live on
Through the stories untold
the power of the unknown and the questions left
Unanswered?
If I die under their command, I have lost.
If my eyes are shut tight in fear, I have lost.
The clandestine destiny demands to take the rest of me,
But I will choose another finale.

# Desperation

I've been thinking a lot lately
about prayers and shadows

The last time I prayed I was asking for you
to turn back time and let your skin have color again
to turn back time and breathe life into your shadow,
dappled and pale, like the memories.
But your hollow heartbeat never left the drum circle
because everywhere I went, memories of you shook my hand.

The last time I prayed, I didn't care that I didn't believe anymore
it was worth a try and worth feeling humiliated,
worth feeling worthless and degraded by my own conscience.
Worth feeling selfish.
You never let me be selfish.

The last time I prayed I felt childish and lost,
murmuring in the dark all those years ago,
the cold, floral pillows beside me laughing,
making fun of the way I said "God"
because they could hear the cobwebs and dust on the letters.

I've been thinking a lot lately,
about desperation and the tap dances we do
to please the crooked versions of ourselves
that only funhouse mirrors and shadows are able to make sense of.

# Apathy

i'd rather feel sadness than nothing at all
but lately its sadness or nothing at all
so what do i do when i feel nothing at all
and i long for sadness
but when the sadness creeps back and hurls me into darkness
all-consuming coldness
aloneness
i long for nothing at all?

# Dark Voice

I count up as I breathe in
And back down as I breathe out
A futile dream of reaching a higher number.

I count up as I breathe in
Chest rising, oxygen intake
Limited in numbers
Limited in time

Limited in time
I count up as I breathe in
Passing each day with newfound
Regret
Never for my actions, for I remain innocent
But regret for having a voice

I regret having a voice that does not work
Because of the color of my skin
I regret having a voice that is engraved with mistakes
Because of the color of my skin

Every part of me has hardened
But my fingertips are soft
The metal strings of my guitar
Ache for my return.

# Shift

I judge a day by the coldness of its shadows,
Where the sun cannot deceive me.
Where rays cannot bend and wash my world with colors who mock me
But where trees and pavilions help to mimic
The Earth's natural state: dark, desolate, iced over
Only thawed and awoken by the sun's garish smile.
Silent, we sit
In the shadows
Feeling the possibilities

# Rehab

Suffocating and shivering
Brow furrowed in pain
Black tears tracing my cheeks
Shallow breathing to slow the pace
Of my heart becoming heavy
Struggling to beat
A tune, off tempo, with a reluctant conductor

# Routine

The exhaustion in your voice
Traipses around the corner
The only proof you stand
Reflected in a shadow
Cast along amber walls, painted over but never cleaned
As practice turns to practice
Patients remain the same
An elevator sounds and you instinctively walk forward
Allow the doors to close
As you blink with memories of results unexpected.

# Buddy

Confusing communication with
        connection
I'm reminded of rejection
        subjection
on your terms,
   well, listen to mine
        You'll be sleeping when you hear them
feel them,
...
in time.

# Unwind

The most sincere lies
Emanate from your eyes
Begging to be believed.

Vaults of secrets come in twos
Thick-rimmed, focused, an unassuming shade of blue.

Stale cigarettes
Cling to your taste buds
Hidden memories peak behind a curtain of teeth,
Like nervous tap dancers at their first recital.

Feel the rhythm of your words
Sense the vibrations; stay on tempo.
Truth telling is an art.
Unwind—
I'll be waiting.

# Masquerades

Truth be told:
You're a liar,

Truth be told:
I look away when I see you
Eyes fleeing from the scene like a criminal
Throat closing like prison doors
Hands shaking like empathetic but distant cousins at your brother's funeral,

Truth be told:
You put up fronts, barricades before a hurricane
You deliver sermons like you're saved but your hypocrisy wears the choir robe,

Truth be told:
Your self-loathing is becoming toxic
Like the cigarettes you smoke in a non-smoking parking lot
Spitting carcinogenic acid in the lungs of the helpless
Who are choking just to say hello.

## Polished Souls

Rented dress shoes, what have you seen?

How many toes have grown cold inside of you;
How many men have stepped down from the altar with you as their guide;
Have you seen death
At a funeral;
Have you seen joy
At a wedding;
Have you been splashed with a tear or a puddle in the rain;
Have you been stepped upon
At an awkward boy's first prom;
Rented dress shoes, what have you seen?
Do you feel the miles
Of each man who claims you as his own for a night;
You come and you see
Silent
Your souls polished like new
Each pair of slacks that rests upon your tongue tastes different
Your shine deceiving each man, who believes you witness his moment
As a virgin.

# Haiku No. 2

Memories of your
hesitant eyes, that don't lin-
-ger, keep me awake

PART II

# See More

Dear ex lover:
When I'm with him, every movement is a mirror image of you. The words I say now are spoken in harmony with my voice of years ago, higher pitched and more sure.
Each syllable flowing like I'm saying it to you, steady and young and unaware
Of pain
Naive of break ups and bad days and nostalgia
The only nostalgia I knew was for the future
But now it's for the first time I said I love you

Ex lover, you lurk behind every guitar string and every pair of circular spectacles.
Images of your skin are etched into my eyes, tattoos, and I search for circles to put your squareness to rest.
But my memory is tainted with so many lyrics and poems and crumpled notes on thin, three-holed paper that no combination of words is left unsaid. I find myself decoding sentences, rearranging them until I have one that you made.
Ex lover I look for you.

I don't remember your taste but I remember your touch,
Passion. I look for your touch.

Ex lover, I can't go on with you sending me songs and reminding me of the afternoon in the park in the back of your car with the CD playing
I can't go on with you reminding me that I used to know how to live
I can't continue being the carcass of myself with you spitting oxygen into my blood and jabbing notes into my heart
Because eventually I will spill.
Eventually I will spill over and leave a mess.
And ex lover, I've used my last napkin to write you this letter.

# Half of Me

The hum of your voice was familiar before I was born.
But it became so foreign when I actually met you.

Things you never taught me, words you never said, places you never were;
Personified in the afterimage of your plate.
        Nature, not nurture, is our only connection,
And your blank stares are not a lesson.
        If you kill all the crows is it still a murder?
...
I slipped a letter under your door
As you slipped pills into your pockets
And slipped into unconsciousness
and later onto the floor,
and into the sheets of your hospital bed.
I looked at those thin white sheets, and pretended we were going to suspend them
from the ceiling
into a fort—
Like the one I wanted to make when I was little,
that you tore down because it was in your way.

You never taught me how to make a white sheet fort
and you never taught me how to love.
all you taught me
was how to walk
away.

You taught me what rejection felt like.
and that if I walked in your bedroom while you were on the phone,
I would be told to keep quiet.
Just like the time I had drawn you a picture.
My little hands still smelled like wax, from the crayons.
I tried to show you but you turned the back of your black swiveling chair
to look me in the face

as warm tears slid down my cheeks.
You taught me rejection.

You taught me that no matter how many words I've heard you speak,
Your voice will never be familiar.

# Resurgence

And you never know how much you mean something
Until you're saying the exact same words, in the same order,
to him—but they sound different.
Dripping with truth and vulnerability and hope,
That they will echo in your direction.

# Timing

Imaginary boy
Where did you hide
When the time was right and the sun had not
Heated the concrete to a temperature
Unbearable for bare feet and bare hearts
To lay themselves down
In the open

# Parallel Universe

You see me cry
But he sees me blush
You see me collapse
But he sees me succeed
You see me, awake and asleep
Struggling for air and masking a history
He sees me laughing and toasting
To a life I don't have
To a story I construct
When I'm with him.

# Queens

Introduce me to your stringless symphony;
Bassless grunge band,
Snareless punk show.
Introduce me to the impossibilities;
Your endless incongruences,
Contradictions that bloom and offer paper scrolls,
Scriptures of truth and belonging.
Introduce me to your world;
Kiss my hand and shake my cheek;
Turn me up and throw me over,

The edge of reality—
And punctual cognizance,
Emblematic prophet,
Blowing smoke rings onto trembling fingers.
Teach me your sober psychedelic language;
Turn back clocks or fast forward to a time when
We can't remember being anything but each other.

# Kings

You slept and awakened a siren
As we sang a siren song
In two beds made to look like one
We wrote a song of regret and lust

# Fade

A shadow of us
Lingers to my right
Watching and judging without any eyes

A shadow of me
Lingers to my right
Footsteps colliding with reversed orientation

Shadows of who we might have been
Disappear with the moonlight
But reemerge daily to torture and corrupt

Grayscale personas, etched with uncertainty
Stalking, watching, mocking

A reflection without expression,
A shadow of you,
A mirage in the distance,
Unreachable, yet touchable,
begins to grow cold.

# Inevitable

Darkness masks expressions
but never intentions

canopies of green and grey hide us from the world.
We retreat to a wooded shelter as
"should" and "should not" go blind
Heavy eyelids and steady gazes reveal
us to ourselves
The reflection in your eyes is of me
and I'm holding your face
My own wide eyes pierce into themselves through
mutual reflection
Mutual recognition, recollection
of the footsteps that led us here
a winding path with shortcuts, always taken
Disillusioned and God forsaken
Dropping words like dice and betting on each other.
Slurring smiles and dancing tongues
deceive the strangers on the roads in their cars,
And the flowers that look up to us.
Rainclouds wash the world and paint a scene for
Celestial spheres, your eyes
Twinkle and dull in pain and delight
Atlas arms, endless spindles of comfort and direction
Reaching out, trunks to branches to twigs to leaves
Fabricating a reality that matches our dreams
creating a life that can be paused and has an off button.
Black and brown on a pallet of color

exchanging *I love you's* and acting like movie stars who are friends with
celebrities,

All the while knowing that every painter
washes out the brushes that have just created
a masterpiece.

# April Showers

Wildflower heart,
Where did you hide?
Amid the weeds and the tall grass
Come out, don't be shy.

Wildflower love,
Who brought you here?
Sprinkled gently alongside the pavement
A gift to observant passers by

Wildflower mind,
What do you ponder?
Unobtrusive, bending in the warm breeze
Petals reaching for the sunlight

## Saying Goodbye

Darling!
Do not look away
We haven't got much time.
Soak in every ounce and every fleeting breath
Every shallow heartbeat that already aches for your return
Stop that!
Your blinks add up
Seconds are being stolen from me
By your greedy eyelids

# Haiku No. 3

Always shaking with
Nervousness or laughter I
Can never tell which

# About the Author

EMILY DALGO is an undergraduate Honors student at American University pursuing a B.A. in international studies with a focus in justice, ethics, and human rights. Dalgo is passionate about social justice advocacy and activism and was awarded the Brady Tyson Award for Excellence in Work Related to Human Rights by the School of International Service in 2016, and is also a 2016 Victor Hassine Memorial Scholar. Dalgo serves as Chief Development Officer at BleakHouse Publishing and has previously been published in *Tacenda Literary Magazine* and *BleakHouse Review*, for which she served as an Associate Editor in 2015.

# About the Artist and Designers

JACOB BRAY graduated from American University in 2016 where he studied political science and fine art. He has contributed illustrations to Bleakhouse and other publications. He currently lives in Washington D.C.

CASEY CHIAPPETTA is an undergraduate honors student majoring in sociology at American University and a widely published author of essays and articles on social justice as well as an accomplished editor and designer. She spent the last year studying social policy at the London School of Economics and working for a UK government scheme to mentor at-risk youth in East London. She spent two months working as an advocate for dialogue in Israel/Palestine during the escalation up to the Gaza War in 2014. She spent three weeks this summer doing the same. Her experience both working in and with conflict resolution strengthened her resolve to fight for social justice, but shifted the focus of her efforts from the international to domestic. Her passion is the study of people and the ways in which different groups interact, particularly with regard to power dynamics.

BILL KAKENMASTER is an undergraduate in the School of International Service at American University pursuing a degree in International Studies. He was previously published in the 2015 *Bleakhouse Review*.

SONIA TABRIZ graduated from American University (2010) *summa cum laude* with University Honors and a B.A. in Law & Society and Psychology. She received the Outstanding Scholarship at the Undergraduate Level award for her award-winning works of fiction, legal commentaries, artwork, presentations, university-wide accolades, and academic achievement. Tabriz went on to attend The George Washington University Law School, where she served as a Writing Fellow and Editor-in-Chief of a law journal. She is now an attorney in the Washington, DC office of a national law firm. Tabriz is the Managing Editor of BleakHouse Publishing and designs the text for various publications.

# Other Titles from BleakHouse Publishing

*Black Bone*, Alexa Marie Kelly

*An Elegy for Old Terrors*, Zoé Orfanos

*Up the River*, Chandra Bozelko

*Distant Thunder*, Charles Huckelbury

*Enclosures: Reflections from the Prison Cell and the Hospital Bed*, Shirin Karimi

*A Zoo Near You*, Robert Johnson et al.

*Origami Heart: Poems by a Woman Doing Life*, Erin George

*Tales from the Purple Penguin*, Charles Huckelbury

*Burnt Offerings*, Robert Johnson

# More Praise for *Silent, We Sit*

The illustration that accompanies Part 1 of Emily Dalgo's fine new volume of poetry resembles the two cerebral hemispheres united by a small hasp and chain. The choice is appropriate; the poems presented demonstrate a remarkable cross lateralization, a union of both existential and artistic sensibility that is evident from the opening haiku and grows stronger until the final poem's speaker confesses an inability to distinguish between "nervousness or laughter."

Ms. Dalgo's collection is rich in texture and revolutionary in the same manner that Twain's magnum opus was revolutionary—both works challenge our placid preconceptions on race, relationships, and criminal justice, daring the reader to think outside our personal comfort zones. "Headlines," for example, revisits the social mask that African Americans must often wear and the safety in ignorance of current events: "[Y]ou couldn't be happy if you read these papers every day."

The book is also an empathetic exercise, demonstrating a remarkable ability of the various speakers to change places with their subjects, as in "Self-Deprecation," a lucid and rich description of the doubt that comes unbidden no matter how substantial the victory. Extending the theme, "Unwind" invokes the imagery of "tap dancers at their first recital" to describe the speaker's awareness of a lover's "most sincere lies" and the reasons for them.

Part 2 opens with another dramatic illustration, a broken mirror that represents shattered illusions and the recognition that effort does not guarantee success. This section includes the extraordinary poem "Half of Me" that merits an extended quote here: "You never taught me how to make a white sheet fort / and you never taught me how to love. / all you taught me / was how to walk / away." This section thus concentrates on both the disappointment and rewards that attend human existence. As Ms. Dalgo, reminds us, "every painter/ washes out the brushes that have just created / a masterpiece." Given the impermanence of our lives, this collection of poems is a welcome tonic to the empty promises and platitudes of the current election cycle, vis-a-vis the reality that every individual must face each morning.

Emily Dalgo's talent and perception are evident from start to finish. Her work is a confrontation of life's fluctuations and a courageous refusal to be broken by them. It is a recognition that the world disappoints but more than that, it is a celebration of the human spirit that can and does overcome those disappointments.

> - Susan Nagelsen, Author, *Exiled Voices: Portals of Discovery – Stories, Poems, and Drama by Imprisoned Writers*

Infrequently a young poet appears with the ability and tools to capture the world we inhabit with such extraordinary detail and perception that the rest of us are left shaking our heads in stunned appreciation. Emily Dalgo is such a poet, and her collection *Silent, We Sit* puts to rest the fallacy that only those who have lived three decades or longer can render what it means to be human in intelligible terms. Ms. Dalgo keeps her unjaundiced eye fixed squarely on both the temporal and the eternal, treating such subjects as personal relationships, the persistence of racism, criminal justice, and the confluence of hope and numbing despair that each of us must encounter at some time during our lives. The speaker in "Apathy," for example, states succinctly, "[I]'d rather feel sadness than nothing at all."

This is not, however, to say that Emily Dalgo's poetry is a simplistic exercise in rejection or dejection. Who can resist a knowing smile when reading "See More," a brief address to an ex-lover, when the speaker says eloquently, "I've used my last napkin to write you this letter." We come away from the poem, and others, wishing that we had perhaps adopted that precise technique in our personal circumstances to convey a sense of relief and finality. Or consider the visceral and tactile combinations in "Timing," in which we are treated to the imagery of heated concrete "Unbearable for bare feet and bare hearts." Or the trenchant comparison of lovers in "Parallel Universe." These are poems of hope, limned perhaps by past tears and fears but nonetheless placed securely in the present, where the goal is to reach the point where "We can't remember being anything but each other."

When asked the difference between a pessimist and an optimist, the coherent response is that the pessimist is the one with the experience. Emily Dalgo lacks the chronological experience to qualify her as a pessimist, and her poems defy any attempt to treat them as cynical observations of the human condition. They are instead remarkable reflections of a flexible and incisive poetic sense that functions, as the poem "Rehab" has it, as "A tune, off tempo, with a reluctant conductor." One hopes that this conductor will soon return to the podium with more music for us to hear.

> - Charles Huckelbury, Senior Consulting Editor of BleakHouse Publishing, Award-Winning Poet and Author of *Tales from the Purple Penguin* and *Distant Thunder*

In *Silent, We Sit*, Emily Dalgo presents emotional truths in plain, bright colors. In Part 1, she goes behind prison bars to depict characters describing the motions of their heart in solitary confinement or when contemplating whether to ask for an expedited execution. Less sensationally, she describes the daily emotions and life rhythms of the condemned, and most important of all, she frames her depiction of the interior life of the imprisoned with two poems in which she contemplates race in the Black Lives Matter era. In Part 2, Dalgo turns a frank gaze on her own travails, mostly about love and broken hearts. Throughout, readers gain a clear look at a society that is blind to the consequences of its behavior.

> - Michael Manson, Director of Undergraduate Research and Integrity, American University

Emily Dalgo's collection is a bold step for a new poet. She considers the intersection between the political and the personal, reckoning each with youthful sincerity. At once provocative and vulnerable, her poetry asks us how we arrived at this moment in time, yet also reminds us that some heartaches are timeless.

> - Cynthia Baer Van Dam, Professor of Writing Studies, American University

Dalgo's debut, *Silent, We Sit*, harnesses the heaviness of the millennial generation. Whether turning her eye to current events or past romances, Dalgo's poetry contains piecing moments of insight. "Silent" reflects deeply on the idea that pain and joy are two sides of the same moment; in the conclusion of "Inevitable" Dalgo writes, "All the while knowing that every painter / washes out the brushes that have just created / a masterpiece." Though many of her poems are painfully present in the "hell" of a hateful, imprisoned society, Dalgo gives us hope. In the final lines of "Shift," she writes, "Silent we sit / In the shadows / Feeling the possibilities." All readers will feel the possibilities of Miss Dalgo's thoughtful words and their power to express the depth of our society's shadows.

- Zoe Orfanos, Author, *An Elegy for Old Terrors*

www.ingramcontent.com/pod-product-compliance
Lightning Source LLC
Chambersburg PA
CBHW052136010526
44113CB00036B/2278